# NOW THAT YOU'RE SAVED

... What happens next?

JAY ZINN

**Now That You're Saved...What Happens Next?**

Copyright © 2019 by Jay Zinn
Published by iZee Books
235 Spinnaker Court
Davidson, NC 28036

**izeebooks.com**

**Cover design** by Jim Xavier
All rights reserved. No part of this publication may be reproduced, stored in a retrieval system or transmitted in any way by any means, electronic, mechanical, photocopy, recording or otherwise, without the prior permission of the publisher, except as provided by USA copyright law.

Printed in the United States of America.

ISBN: 978-1-0713848-4-8

# CONTENTS

| | |
|---|---|
| Who is Jesus? | 10 |
| Why did Jesus come? | 12 |
| Discovering what God is like | 15 |
| What is the Bible? | 16 |
| False "gods" or the true God | 18 |
| Jesus stands apart as God above all gods | 20 |
| The pivotal point in history—His-Story | 22 |
| Setting things right with God | 24 |
| Show us the Father | 25 |
| His trial, death, & resurrection | 26 |
| Everyone dies—then the afterlife | 27 |
| Living stones—Children of light—People of the Way | 28 |
| Holy Spirit and the "triune" mystery | 31 |
| The mind of Christ and our "aha" moments | 33 |
| A new person, a new creation, an exchanged life | 35 |
| Radical change in other areas | 37 |
| The spirit whisperer | 41 |
| Here's what happens | 43 |
| Resisting the temptation to sin | 44 |
| Jesus will return to resurrect us from the grave | 47 |
| What is the evidence of a person's salvation? | 48 |
| Church attendees or faith producers? | 51 |
| Finishing the race you started | 53 |
| Honest sinner or deceived pretender? | 55 |
| Life and Lip | 59 |
| Reading the four gospels | 61 |
| Not overnight, but a "process" | 63 |
| Your "quiet" place | 65 |
| Church attendance—is it enough? | 68 |
| Other steps—water baptism and Spirit baptism | 70 |
| Saved to be fruit-bearing disciples | 74 |
| Not for the faint of heart | 76 |
| Run well | 80 |

# Introduction

In a time of easy believism, where becoming a Christian seems as simple as going forward after an invitation to "get saved," it is possible that some may have prayed a prayer to "accept" Christ but have not been saved or "born again" the way the Bible explains it.

After they've prayed for salvation, many converts are left without follow up or anything that could speak to the genuineness of their experience. They might have accepted the fact of Christ's existence, or acknowledged their need for salvation, but how can they be certain they were actually saved? Where is the evidence of their conversion? What is different now to show that they're a new creation?

During my trip to Asia in 2018, I preached to an underground church of about one hundred members in attendance. I was concerned for those who had come forward for salvation because the leaders did not have a plan in place for follow-up due to the oppressive government monitoring of "unlicensed" churches by the government.

When these hungry souls came in front of the congregation, they received a written prayer and prayed in unison. They were then embraced by everyone and sent home—most of whom would never be seen again. This troubled me.

During my fifteen days there, I had a lot of down time, as my job was to keep out of sight of the government's watchful eye. I decided to use this unexpected time to write this very booklet so that I would be able to put something in the hands of those who were praying to receive Christ but weren't able to also receive the needed follow-up.

Though I wrote this book for the church in China, it's applicable to everyone, everywhere. It is important for new converts, regardless of the culture or country they live in, to know what they've signed up for. In nations especially hostile toward Christians, it becomes even more important to understand that there's a cost that comes with their conversion, a price that should never be sugar-coated by the church fearing the truth-seeking candidate might change their mind.

It's my prayer that this little book goes around the world to prepare new believers with a solid foundation of knowledge for *what happens next*. And may the church rise up to assist them with this important consideration—that a heart changed by God changes a life and is not only the evidence of *true* repentance, but of becoming a new creation in Christ.

*The Author*

# Now That You're Saved ...What Happens Next?

Now that you've prayed and asked Jesus to save you, what does that mean for you? For your life? Becoming a follower of Christ is a serious decision and it is not one to be taken lightly.

What do you need to know about starting this journey?

This book is designed to help give you a glimpse into what you can expect in both your relationship with Jesus and in understanding the importance of who he is.

As you read, I would encourage you to underline or circle any words and phrases that pull at your heart. This gentle tug will be your spirit resonating with the Holy Spirit as he highlights relevant points in the moment. I also recommend that you read this book several times as you will see something new and more clearly each time.

## Who is Jesus?

We must begin with this question because it was the most significant question Jesus presented to his disciples:

*"Who do **you** say that I am?"*

Simon Peter replied, *"You are the Christ (Messiah), the Son of the living God."*[1]

Jesus Christ, the Son of God, is the single most influential figure throughout all of time, therefore it is important to know *who* he is and *what* that means for us.

His life was and is so powerful that the calendar we use today was established by his birth-the pivotal point in history. No one else can lay claim to defining the world's calendar by which

---

[1] Matthew 16:13-17

every nation determines and chronicles the activities of their days, weeks, months and years.

Jesus is neither a myth nor the fabrication of some eastern or western culture. There are more written documents from eyewitness accounts about his life, death and resurrection than any other person or event in history.

Jesus isn't another "god" added to other religious systems in countries where people worship a host of deities. He is *the* God above all gods. And as God himself (the second member of the Trinity[2]), he took on human flesh at God's predetermined time, coming to live among us.

Though born in the form of a man, Jesus came from *another* world—not another planet but another realm called the *third* heaven. He claimed this

---

[2] The Christian **doctrine** of the **Trinity** (Latin: Trinitas, lit. 'triad', from Latin: trinus "threefold") holds that God is one God, but **three** coeternal consubstantial persons or hypostases—the Father, the Son (Jesus Christ), and the Holy Spirit—as "one God in **three** Divine Persons".

repeatedly about himself. He was "*other*-worldly." A light who came to shine in a world immersed in darkness.

## Why did Jesus come?

Jesus came to reveal the one and only true God who is the Maker of all living things. He declared that he alone is the *way*, the *truth* and the *life*—i.e., the only way anyone can to come to the Father. The Father, God, made his Son, Jesus, king and ruler over every kingdom and nation on earth. But when he came, the world didn't recognize or receive him as such.

And though he was Israel's king, Jesus didn't come into the world as a fully formed adult to take his rightful place by force as other kings had done. Instead, he arrived in Bethlehem as a baby, born of the Virgin Mary who was married to Joseph.

At his birth there was no royal fanfare, no earthly celebration, and no grand entrance. He laid in a straw-packed feeding trough for a crib with Mary and Joseph at his side, and a handful of shepherds sent by angels to come welcome him. Jesus came as God wrapped in the flesh of a human infant.

He grew up in a small town called Nazareth, 80 miles north of Jerusalem, where he lived in obscurity as a humble carpenter until the day God the Father revealed him to the world.

At the age of thirty, Jesus stepped into the waters of the River Jordan to be baptized by his cousin, John. The Holy Spirit descended upon him in the form of a dove and then led him into the desert for forty days and nights to be tested by the devil.

When he returned victorious from his test, he didn't round up an army or lead a rebellion against Rome. Instead, he gathered twelve disciples to himself and started a revolution of the heart to turn people back to God.

As Israel's legitimate king by pedigree, Jesus came to insert a *heavenly* kingdom into the earthly kingdoms of this world. He invited the children of Israel to become citizens of the kingdom he had brought from another dimension, which is why he repeatedly said, *"The kingdom of heaven is at hand."*

Sent by the Father, Jesus came to liberate God's tarnished creation from the sin of Adam [3]—the first man God created. What Adam forfeited in his act of disobedience, Jesus came to recover, but not without a price. He came to redeem [4] everyone from Adam's folly through the sacrifice of his own life. He laid down his life for ours.

The blood he shed on the cross was the ransom [5] note he paid in exchange for our sins so that we could stand before a holy God, as newly adopted members into his family in heaven and on earth.

---

[3] **Adam** was the first man God created and had disobeyed God's express command to not eat from the fruit of the tree of knowledge of good and evil (Genesis 2-3). His disobedience brought sin and death into the world, as well as a curse upon the earth.

[4] **redeem**—to buy back what has been lost, stolen, or forfeited to another.

[5] **ransom**—payment or payoff to cancel the debt owed for Adam's sin and ours.

Your prayer of salvation was an *act* of faith. If your prayer was genuine, then not only was the debt of all your sins canceled by his blood, you are no longer a slave to sin and your whole life—body, soul and spirit—has been purchased by that blood to become *his* slave. In reality, it was his life in exchange for yours.

Before you prayed, you were subject to sin as your slave master. But by making Jesus your Lord and Savior you transferred the ownership of your life entirely over to him. Jesus now owns you as a servant in his household and as a citizen of his kingdom, which he wants to *visibly* manifest through you. Another world has entered your heart—the world of heaven's kingdom is now at your disposal, waiting to be unpacked to reveal the contents of its bountiful treasures.

## Discovering what God is like

So how do you get your hands on the treasures and riches of the King's domain? How do you discover what it's like to be a citizen of his kingdom? How do you learn the principles and values that run it?

Discovering this new life begins by making every effort to read and study the life and teachings of Jesus Christ. These teachings are found in the first four books of the New Testament. They're called the *gospels*.[6]

Every kingdom reflects the nature of its king—i.e., *who* he is and *what* he is like. As soon as you get a Bible for yourself, you'll have God's Word as a teacher and a guide. If you want to know what God is like, look at Jesus' life.

## What is the Bible?

The Bible[7] is a library of 66 books divided into two distinct sections:

The **Old Testament**—comprised of **39 books**
The **New Testament**—comprised of **27 books**

It is a compilation of divinely inspired books that chronicle the history

---

[6] **Gospel**-means good news.
[7] The word "**Bible**" comes from the Greek word *Biblion*, which means "**book**."

of the world. Reading through the Bible will walk you through creation, the first man and woman, the entrance of sin into the world and the fallout from sin. You will also see the manifestation of sin in an ongoing war of the gods [8] and kingdoms of this world against the kingdom of God and his covenant [9] people.

Part of your new adventure in Christ's kingdom includes discovering what God is like. Everything hinges on this. The Bible reveals God's nature and his multifaceted attributes, many of

---

[8] **gods**—a reference in the Bible to fallen angels or spiritual beings created by God before he created man. A rebellion against God was led by the devil (also known as Lucifer), a chief divine being among other angelic creatures who fell from his place in heaven when pride and sin was found in him (Isaiah 14: 12-14; Ezekiel 28:12-17).

[9] **covenant**—a contract initiated by God to his people for the purpose of sustaining an abiding relationship between them which would insure divine protection and provision by God, as long the people did not break the terms of the contract ratified by the blood of animal sacrifices and ultimately the blood of God's own Son, Jesus Christ.

which are discovered in the biblical record of his dealings with humanity since the beginning of time.

Throughout the Old Testament we see a sequence of historical events, prophecies and covenants that demonstrate God's plan to redeem the world back to himself through Jesus Christ. The New Testament is the last and crowning covenant of all previous Old Testament covenants, as they have now been fulfilled in Christ.

The New Testament includes the arrival of Christ's birth, his public ministry, and the *new* covenant he established between God and his church made possible through his death and resurrection.

The word "church" means *called-out ones. The church* is universally composed of Jews and Gentiles (non-Jewish nations) who together are bound to this *new* covenant and their king—Jesus Christ the Son of God.

## False "gods" or the true God

As mentioned earlier, you might come from a culture that worships other gods. Perhaps your ancestors worshiped and served gods through the idols they fashioned into wood. Maybe it was stone images they perceived their god or gods to be like. Either way, these gods were likely fashioned based upon what these gods were believed to be able to do.

Most people are unaware of the *unseen* realm of spiritual beings which inhabit idols and influence those who worship them. People who prefer to follow the gods of their ancestors might ask, *"Who is Jesus anyway? What sets him apart from our father's god(s)? What makes him better than the gods of my forefathers?"*

What they don't realize is that these other gods are counterfeit heralds of a false and misleading message from the devil (Lucifer). These gods are incapable of doing what their prophets, mediums, witchdoctors, priests or mediators promise to those who believe in them.

The most important thing a person could ever hope to gain, their gods cannot provide because they're incapable of it. They cannot atone[10] for or deliver anyone from their sins, and therefore, cannot offer eternal life with God in the afterlife. Only Jesus can do that.

The gods—which attach themselves to idols of the nations that worship them—are created spiritual beings who left their first estate when they followed the devil into a rebellion against God, which resulted in them being cast from his presence. They forfeited their allotted assignments in service to their Creator and are now fallen beings from the *unseen* realm. This means that they are ultimately reserved for the lake of fire, along with everyone else who rebels against God, or continues to worship these gods.

## Jesus stands apart as God above all gods

---

[10] To **atone for**—means to make amends: to provide or serve as reparation or compensation for something bad or unwelcome.

Unlike these fallen spiritual beings, Jesus stands above them all because he is not *a* god, he *is* God. And he is fully able to provide eternal life to those who believe in him.

As a newly adopted member into Christ's kingdom and household, you must abandon the gods of your fathers, remove all idols and idolatrous practices from your life and align your trust and loyalty with King Jesus. You cannot serve two masters. Either your former gods (or god) is your god or Jesus is your God. You can't have both. You must choose Jesus above all gods.

Jesus is God's only begotten Son and, *as* God, by him and for him all things were created in heaven and earth. This includes the visible and the invisible, including every spiritual being in the invisible realm that fell from grace in the rebellion led by Lucifer.

The Jewish religious leaders of the day knew about these other gods from the Scriptures in the first of the Ten Commandments. God told his people, *"I am the Lord your God, ...You shall have no other gods before me."* Because Jesus claimed godhood and equality with God the Father, they concluded that he must be a false god endeavoring to lead people away from the Law of Moses and the one and only true God of Israel. So they crucified him on charges of blasphemy against God.

Jesus never said he was *a* god. He said he *was* God—the "I AM" of Israel. To the religious leaders this was disrespectful and made a mockery of God. By saying this, Jesus provoked them to fulfill the plan God determined before the foundation of the world—i.e., that Jesus would redeem all who received him by the shedding of his spotless, sinless blood, the blood that would atone for and cancel our debt of sin.

## The pivotal point in history—His-Story

As mentioned earlier, the Old Testament is made up of God-initiated *covenants* with the patriarchs, with Moses, and with Israel. But Israel failed to keep the terms of these covenants during the time of their existence.

As a covenant people under the Law of Moses, they were destined to become a "kingdom of priests" who would turn nations away from their *gods* to the Creator and God of all, the God of their forefathers: Abraham, Isaac, and Jacob.

The children of Israel, however, repeatedly disobeyed God's laws that were meant to set them apart from the wicked cultures and gods of other nations. Generation after generation rejected God's laws until he finally rejected them and the perpetual cycle of their incurable disobedience.

They were still his people, but they were incapable of serving him with their whole heart, soul, and body. Knowing this would happen—before the foundation of the world—God had a plan in place to set things right through the only person in history who could do so—Jesus Christ his Son.

The law, the psalms, and the prophets in the Old Testament all pointed toward this time in history—the arrival of the Messiah. This is why history is all about HIS-story.

From 4004 B.C. to 4 B.C., we look *forward* to Christ's birth.

From today's date A.D. to 30 A.D., we look *backwards* to Christ's death and resurrection.

All history pivots on the life and times of Jesus Christ until the day he returns for all who have accepted and believed in him—just as you have done.

## Setting things right with God

By his death, Jesus came to set things right between us and God. Humanity couldn't do it, false gods could never do it, and religion couldn't do it. Only God the Son—who became a man—could fulfill all of heaven's requirements to bridge the gap between God and us (his fallen creation).

Because Jesus came to earth as 100 percent God and 100 percent man (without sin or a sin nature) his body could be offered to God as a blameless, righteous, sinless sacrifice for the sins that have kept us separated from a relationship with a holy, righteous God.

Jesus came with the mission of removing the death penalty that is hanging over our heads by dying in our place. There's no greater love that could be shown by any person, even if undeserved.

## Show us the Father

Besides taking our sins upon himself (when he hung on the cross), Jesus came to show us what God the Father was like. He came as the exact reflection of the Father's love, kindness, and mercy. That's why he said to his disciple, Thomas, *"He who has seen me, has seen the Father."*

Though Jesus is *not* the Father, he did only what the Father told him to do so that in everything he did, whether in word or deed, he was the divine expression of *who* and *what* the Father in heaven was like. You'll see this demonstrated when you read the gospel accounts of Jesus' life on earth in the New Testament.

## His trial, death, and resurrection

At the end of three-and-a-half years of public ministry, Jesus was arrested by the religious authorities and tried in an illegal court procedure for blasphemy against God and treason against Caesar. They manipulated the Roman governor, Pilate, to beat him, scourge him mercilessly with the flagella[11] and crucify him on a hill called Calvary, just outside of Jerusalem. Jesus hung on the cross for six hours in unbearable pain until, at three in the afternoon, he breathed his last and died.

That same day his mother and friends took his body from the cross and buried him in the borrowed tomb of a rich man named Joseph of Arimathea.

Three nights and three days later, Jesus rose from the grave, just as he had predicted. He rose not only to demonstrate power and authority over hell, death and the grave, but to offer

---

[11] **flagella** — a Roman whip called the "cat of nine tails" made with leather strands imbedded with shards of sharp steel intended to rip the skin.

himself to God as the first fruit of the resurrection of the saints, going as far back as Adam.

## Everyone dies—then the afterlife

Adam and Eve had *immortal* bodies until their disobedience in Genesis 3 brought sin and death into their lives. This was passed down to their offspring, including all of us.

And since everyone dies, every soul will pass through death's door into the afterlife, either in a perpetual state of eternal separation *from* God, or eternal life *with* God.

Regrettably, most souls born into the world will reject Christ's offer to save them and throw away their only hope for redemption. By their refusal to believe in Christ and receive the work on the cross he accomplished, they'll choose eternal separation *from* God with no chance of reversing their decision after they die.

Separation from God eternally is bad enough, but to add eternal damnation and the lake of fire for sins committed against God is unimaginable. If we choose to carry the burden and history of our sins to the grave with us, rather than letting Jesus shoulder that burden through the cross, then we've chosen to gamble with the eternal state and condition of our souls.

In blindness and folly, people will reject the only thing that can grant them right-standing with God in the afterlife— that is, the sinless, perfect blood of Jesus Only the blood of Jesus—and no other blood—permits us to stand before God without fear or condemnation. We can only exist before a holy God when we are cloaked in *Christ's* garment of righteousness and the redemptive work, he, and *only* he, could complete on the cross. Jesus is God come in the flesh, with a sinless life and stainless blood that can conquer sin and death.

## Living stones—Children of light— People of the Way

As a "born-again" believer, you're now a child of God the Father. He's adopted you into his family—the church, which isn't a building of brick and mortar, but of "living" stones (his people) fitly joined together.

As mentioned earlier, the word "church" in its original language means *called-out ones*—i.e., a people "called out of" darkness into his marvelous light. We are children of light and our names have been registered in Christ's book of life with our other family members, named in heaven and on earth.

As a child of God, you're a citizen in God's kingdom and a co-heir with Jesus your King. As a subject in his kingdom, you must come to know, apply and practice his teachings, commandments and principles, as they are required of every member in his kingdom.

It's a *new* way of life, different than any you've known from your cultural roots. That's why Christians in the early church were referred to as people of "the Way," meaning *his* way, people who imitated their King, embraced his worldview and stood radically apart from the world.

As a kingdom citizen, you're left *in* this world but no longer *of* this world, or "*other*-worldly" like Jesus. This change happens through the process of surrendering every area of your life to him as your Lord and Master, not only as your Savior.

If you were truly "born again"—when you asked Jesus to save you—you'll stand apart from the world as a *new creation*. And though you're a citizen of your own country here on earth, you also possess a "dual" citizenship by adding the citizenship you now have in Christ's kingdom.

You've signed up to make Jesus Lord and King of your life. Your old thoughts will be replaced with *his* thoughts. Your old ways will be replaced with *his* ways. Not by the power of your will—but from the life of the Holy Spirit who has moved into your spirit to become your guide and teacher.

To grow in *his* ways, focus your efforts on getting to know Jesus. You do this through reading about him in the four gospels of the New Testament. It's in his life where you'll see the exact representation of who and what God is like.

## Holy Spirit and the "triune" mystery

In return for making Jesus Lord and Master, God gives you a new heart to help you walk in the new way of kingdom living and the Holy Spirit. He is the third member of the triune God, and will become your permanent friend and counselor for life.

As Jesus is a person and the Father is a person, the Holy Spirit, too, is a person. In the Bible you'll discover that God is *three* persons (united in *one* purpose) as God the Father, God the Son and God the Holy Spirit. Three-in-one. This characteristic as a three-in-one (triune) God is one of his great *mysteries*.

Similar to God's triune nature, we were designed by him with three indivisible parts—i.e., a *body*, a *soul* and a *spirit*.

Our **body** is the temporal earthly tent (or house) of our soul and spirit. It is the "***world*-conscious**" part of our being.

Our **soul** is eternal and is the "***self*-conscious**" part of our being. It is our mind, will and emotions.

Our **spirit** is also eternal and is the "***God*-conscious**" or "interior" part of our being which connects us with God. Before salvation, our spirit was void and empty of God's presence, crying out to discover and connect with our Creator. For the lost and unsaved, its voice will never be silenced, and its longing never quenched until Jesus is made Lord and Savior and the Holy Spirit moves into their spirit as their Comforter, Teacher and Guide.

In time, you'll be able to accept this by faith and the witness of the Holy Spirit in you, who will help you see references (by implication) to God's triune nature throughout the Bible. No one, however, can ever fully grasp the magnitude or mechanics of it intellectually, which is what makes it a mystery.

There will be a certain cloud of "unknowing" between us and God because he'll reveal some of his divine attributes, but never all of them, because it's too awesome, too incredible, too magnificent for our finite brains to comprehend all that God is and all that God does.

You will grow in knowing him, but you will never exhaust discovering the limitless capabilities of his personhood and power.

## The mind of Christ and our "aha" moments

The Holy Spirit's work is to help you access the "mind of Christ" when you expose yourself to the readings and teachings of the Bible. The Bible will come alive—living and breathing—as you read each page with an open heart to the revelations of the Holy Spirit.

I recommend you begin with the gospel of John in the New Testament. Take a pen or highlighter and underline or block everything that jumps out at you as an "aha" moment. Especially the words of Jesus.

The "aha" moments may come not only when you're reading the Bible, but also through a good Christian book, a devotional or a message you hear at church. When you read or hear a verse or a quote, you might think, *"Hey, that feels right to my spirit, my interior connection to God! I'm going to ponder that for a while and consider how I can apply it to my life!"*

An "aha" moment like this is the Holy Spirit's nudge for you to take what you've heard or read in your Bible and live it out as a citizen in Christ's kingdom.

In his kingdom, Jesus teaches his citizens to love their enemies, which is a pretty radical principle. So take on your King's mind in that and do it! The Holy Spirit will help you.

Jesus teaches his citizens to forgive each other and anyone who tries to hurt us. Again, radical. Take on his mind in that and do it! The Holy Spirit will help you.

Jesus teaches his citizens to serve and help others, as opposed to being *self*-centered. To take on the King's mind in that is radical, too, because he didn't come like other kings to be served, but as a king who would serve others.

## A new person, a new creation, an exchanged life

The Holy Spirit will regularly give you downloads of "aha" moments to teach you the Lord's ways. He'll give you the *ability* to walk them out and say no to the temptation of sinful ways you once practiced.

Now that you're saved, you're going to notice things that'll make the Holy Spirit uncomfortable. Your spirit (your interior self) will become unsettled and convicted. Your loving Father uses conviction as a powerful tool to help you grow into the *new person* you are in Christ, no longer walking in the Adamic ways of the world. You are now a child of light in the darkness, even while you're still in this world—whether at home, among friends or in the place you work.

Let his light shine through you, not only by the words you declared to serve Christ, but by a life radically altered to reflect the divine nature of Jesus in you. And the Holy Spirit will inspire you to clean up.

By *radically altered,* I mean radically changed from the salty, crude vocabulary you once had.

Radically altered from an edgy sarcasm, replaced with kind, complimentary words that Jesus would say.

Radically altered from a sour countenance to a countenance of joy like Jesus had.

Radically altered from a volatile temper to the calm, patient, disposition Jesus displayed among his disciples.

As your Father's child of light, you can let that light shine brightly through you by the unconditional love of the Holy Spirit, which is activated in you toward others. He'll give you *his* capacity to express genuine, authentic love toward everyone, whether they deserve it or not. This supernatural love is well beyond your natural ability because it is other-worldly. It's *his* love activated in you.

This *new* type of love will not only surprise you, but it is clear evidence that you've been born again.

When people notice these changes and ask what's happened to you—tell them you received Christ's payment for your sins on the cross and you now belong to him and his family.

Tell them any change they see in you is the by-product of *his* life exchanged for your life. Only Jesus can be and do the things that are happening in you.

**Radical change in other areas**

Here are other examples of radical changes the Holy Spirit will help you with. *If* you surrender to the convicting nudge, he'll press upon you to remove certain areas of sin and compromise contrary to God's laws.

For example, if you were involved in any form of substance abuse (i.e., alcohol, drugs or nicotine) the Holy Spirit will be your source of strength to turn from these vices and make your body a clean temple for the Lord.

If you were involved in sexual addictions such as pornography, homosexuality, sex outside of marriage (i.e., fornication), adultery or any other type of sexual addiction, the Holy Spirit will convict you of this, too, because the Bible teaches that those who practice such things cannot inherit his kingdom.[12]

These corruptive activities indulged in by the world will cause your redeemed body (the Lord's temple) to become polluted, defiled and unfit for being an effective witness for him.

The Bible teaches the sinful things engaged in by the world will lead to their destruction. Therefore, these should not be found among God's citizens who are

---

[12] 1 Corinthians 6:9-11

called to imitate the life of their King. Jesus never engaged in any of these sins.

Does this seem difficult to comprehend? Does this cause you to reconsider the commitment you made to God? I only ask because it's *not* easy being a Christian. We still possess a sin nature that our salvation doesn't remove. What our salvation does remove, however, is the strength and power the sin nature once had in ruling our lives.

We've been set free from yielding the members of our body to the lusts of sin, so the Adamic nature can no longer control our passions. Sin no longer *reigns*, but it still *remains* in the members of our body to entice us to yield to its desires. The good news is, with the Holy Spirit residing within our spirit man (interior), all of sin's enticements can be overcome as long as we let Jesus have *all* of our life—not parts of it—and we allow *his* righteous nature to manifest itself through us.

Being a Christian isn't easy because it's a daily *choice* to turn away from everything the Bible calls *sin*. We can do it because Jesus gave us the complete package. He conquered all sin on the cross.

You have access to all the power and authority his victory had gained for you through his death and resurrection. You've been taken captive in his victory train of righteousness, so much so that you can ride on the strength of that victory for the rest of your life. There's absolutely nothing you can't conquer that's been a stronghold in your life if you stay on that train.

The Bible says you can do *all* things through Christ who strengthens you. You're *more* than a conqueror through Christ who loves you—a conqueror over all opposition, temptation, persecution and sin. In all these things he'll give you victory through his name, *if* you choose to daily embrace and release his new nature that is now living in you.

It's a daily choice to confess and repent of sins we commit. Consider it a gift from God whenever the Holy Spirit taps the door of your conscience about sin. He does so to remind you of the victory you already have over that sin through the cross.

Allow the Holy Spirit to help you overcome.

## The spirit whisperer

Going forward in your newfound faith, the Holy Spirit will faithfully whisper in your conscience and nudge your spirit for any sinful actions you might commit in thought, word or deed. He won't *condemn* you; he'll inspire you to recognize that it isn't spiritually healthy for you.

I recognized this immediately upon my own conversion. There were things I did previously that now—as a born-again believer—pricked my conscience when I repeated them.

I discovered two things in this. First, I felt uneasy about doing the same things I did before I was saved which, at the time, seemed normal.

Second, I felt the grace and God-infused desire to quit repeating these actions and change my habits. For example, I immediately eliminated words in my vocabulary that seemed unsuitable for a citizen of Christ's kingdom. No one told me. I just knew in my spirit. I wanted to please God with my words and make them appropriate words.

Whenever this inward prod of the Holy Spirit's conviction happens to you, respond immediately. Acknowledge the sin by confessing it to God and repent. Ask Jesus to forgive you of the sin and then, with the Holy Spirit's help, remove the habit from your life. The blood of Jesus will wash that sin away, and your slate will be clean again.

If, however, you ignore the repeated prodding's of conviction by the Holy Spirit and willfully walk in your habitual sins, a fortified wall of bricks will pile up around your heart (layer by layer) until it becomes a stronghold of justifications for continuing in the sin.

Sadly, if this goes on, it will create in your heart a feeling of separation from God. Not on his part, but because *you* feel uncomfortable around him and the holiness of his being.

**Here's what happens**

When you get to that place of uncomfortableness with God, the Holy Spirit's voice can no longer penetrate your wall (or stronghold) of lies erected between you and God. They're lies that say, *"It's okay for me to do this"* or *"God knows my weakness in this area"* or *"God's grace will cover this because I'm only human."*

When there's no capacity for conviction (a prick in your conscience of wrongdoing), there's no capacity for repentance, and without repentance, there's no opportunity for the Holy Spirit to help you change. The Holy Spirit will not force us to change. He'll invite us to, but we choose whether or not to let him help us toward that change.

Once a person reaches a point of no conviction of the Holy Spirit penetrating their heart, they'll be uncomfortable around God's people, leave the church family, stop praying and stop reading the Bible. They'll also cease to partner with God in the process of the transformation intended for them as they drew closer to him.

This isn't a state of mind you arrive at overnight, but the deception is subtly progressive and can overtake you in the same way it did Adam and Eve. They walked and talked with God in the garden every day. But the serpent in that garden lied to them and invited them to become a *god* to themselves—if they ate from the forbidden fruit. They were enticed to have their *own* throne. So will you if you take his bait of deception to have your *own* throne and be your *own* god, just as you were before you were saved.

**Resisting the temptation to sin**

To repent means: "To have a *change* of mind or a *change* of direction." When God calls us to repentance, he is calling us to turn from strongholds of sin in our lives and rely on the Holy Spirit to help us resist these temptations in the future.

If you fall into the same habit of sin as before, then repeat the process of *acknowledging*, *confessing* and *repenting* of that sin as many times as it takes to defeat the habit and stop going after it.

To help strengthen this method of tearing down strongholds, look up verses in the Bible that carry the word or words that describe the kind of sin that keeps entangling you. Words such as *bitterness*, *unforgiveness*, *greed*, *covetousness*, *sexual impurity*, *fornication*, *strong drink*, or any other type of sin, you can find through Bible apps on your phone or Bible programs online.

When you find the most applicable verses to your sins, write them down in a journal and memorize them. Next time the temptation to sin in that area comes around, speak and declare those verses against that stronghold.

When the devil comes knocking at your door to deliver another brick of lies to place in your wall of sinful habits (those areas where he knows you're weak), tell him he's got the wrong address and slam the door in his face.

Jesus was tempted by the devil just as Adam and Eve were, but he didn't fail his test like they did. Three times he resisted the devil who tempted him in the wilderness *before* the reveal of his public ministry. He defeated him by quoting Scriptures (see Luke 4:1-13). So when you're tempted, remember Jesus was tempted too. Every Christian is tempted to sin. But it's not a sin to be tempted. It wasn't a sin for Jesus to be tempted. It's only a sin when you flirt with temptation long enough to give in to it and carry out the deed.

Reject the temptation immediately, resist the devil, submit to God and run from it. Do this until the devil decides you won't accept his lies and goodies anymore and he'll leave you alone—like he left Jesus alone when he couldn't get him to take the bait.

The devil won't leave you alone indefinitely, however, because he'll send his demonic cohorts to tempt you in *other* areas of weakness. When that happens, repeat the same action of finding verses for that sin, quote them to the devil, resist the devil and look to God for help to turn away and flee from it.

It would also be wise to include a trusted friend to pray with you and be accountable to them when they ask about it. Two are better than one when facing a battle against sin.

## Jesus will return to resurrect us from the grave

When you asked Jesus to save you, you chose the way to a resurrected life. At the end of the age when he comes back to judge the world, he is going to set up his kingdom on earth, removing sin, Satan, sinners and all devils from the world.

When the Lord descends from his throne in heaven, he'll call you up from the grave clothed with an immortal body—a young adult body without a sin nature. You'll rise to meet Jesus in the air along with all the other saints in heaven who died before you. Saints from the Old Testament and the New

Testament who faithfully honored the terms of the covenants God made for them in their day will join together, having full access to him, as they live with him throughout eternity.

This is our hope.

We have this to look forward to.

A new life in the age to come.

## What is the evidence of a person's salvation?

The Bible says *if* we belong to Christ, *if* we're truly saved ("born again"), we'll know we have come to know him *if* we obey his commands. The man or woman who says, "I *know* him," but doesn't do what Jesus commands, is a liar and the truth is not in them. But if anyone *obeys* his word, God's love is truly made complete in them.[13]

This is how we know we are *in* him and that he is *in* us. Whoever claims to live *in* Christ, will make every effort to imitate the love, the life and the moral

---

[13] 1 John 2:3-5a

standards that Jesus displayed in his own life when he walked on earth.[14]

But some will ask, "Doesn't Jesus love us unconditionally, whether we sin or not?"

This is true, because our salvation is not *merit*-based, it's *faith*-based. But he doesn't want us to keep sinning and take advantage of his grace.

The love I have for my children isn't earned by their deeds, but because they're my flesh and blood. My love for them is unconditional, but that doesn't mean I'm okay with them doing bad things.

Like Christ, we demonstrate unconditional love toward others—not by condoning their sin, but by seeing their deepest need for God behind the sin that has them bound and broken, and then doing what we can to help them get delivered from it, beginning with leading them to Christ.

The best evidence of our salvation isn't seeing what we can get away with

---

[14] 1 John 2:5b-6

and then hoping God's love will cover it. Instead, we imitate the life of Jesus because it is *his* life being manifested in and through our life.

For example:

Did Jesus live a life engaged in sexual immorality?

No.

Then, neither should we—because Jesus *in* us would never engage in sexual immorality. We're yielding to *Christ's* nature, not our old Adamic nature from which we've been set free.

Did Jesus lie, commit adultery, steal, cheat or deceive?

No.

Then, neither should we—because Jesus *in* us would never engage in such activity. The person truly born again is given the grace to supernaturally yield to *Christ's* manifested nature in us, not our old Adamic nature from which we've been set free.

Did Jesus live sacrificially, unselfishly, forgive people, love people, empower people, feed the hungry, help the poor, visit those in prison, comfort the weak and do to others as he wanted them to do to him?

Absolutely, he did!

Then so should we, because the Holy Spirit will supernaturally help us imitate *Christ* in all these ways—*if* we allow him to and *if* we surrender to his help to do so. Our obedience to our Father's commands and Christ's teachings will *release* supernatural grace and faith in us to walk in the moral standards that God requires of all his kingdom citizens.

## Church attendees or faith producers?

As a new member in the family, society and culture of heaven's kingdom, your mission is to reflect the life and ways of your King.

We've been created by God and saved by Christ's death to mirror his *devotion* and his *godly behavior* before the Father.

You'll know the Holy Spirit lives inside you when you feel convicted about any sinful habit you practiced before you were saved. If you're not convicted about such sins and choose only to stop some of them (or very little of them), there's a strong possibility your prayer of salvation was either a half-hearted commitment to God, or you didn't understand the cost of becoming a disciple of Jesus. Many in his day didn't count the cost either, though he repeatedly challenged the curious crowd of admirers with the cost of discipleship.

If this seems too much to ask of you, and you thought you were only joining a church (like joining a club) or adding another *god* or *religion* to your list of spiritual experiences, then you've yet to grasp the significance behind asking Jesus to save you. Your salvation isn't about having *religion* in your life, it's about a *relationship* with the Father in heaven and serving him in his kingdom purposes.

I wrote this book to help you understand the enormity of your decision to follow Christ and to explain the depth of what Jesus requires of everyone who wants to become a true Christian.

There are many who think they're Christians because they attend weekly church services. But are they making a dent against the activities of the kingdom of darkness going on around them? Are they a threat to the devil and his minions?

Becoming a follower of Christ doesn't stop at believing in Jesus. The devils believe in Jesus too. It doesn't stop at praying a prayer of faith. Faith *produces* something. It's not passive, but *active*. Healthy, active faith *grows*. It brings about such change in a person's life that it has the power to make hell tremble.

**Finishing the race you started**

I ran cross-country in high school. Each race would be a grueling pace of two to three miles over hills and rough terrain, ending at the quarter-mile track at the school.

Standing at the starting line was *not* the race. Once the gun popped, we took off with every intention of going the distance and crossing the finish line.

In the same way, your prayer of salvation has merely brought you to the starting line of a *heavenly* race on earth. It's going to be a grueling pace across hills and valleys in the spiritual realm.

Starting the race isn't what counts in God's kingdom. What counts is to finish it through the strength and power of the Holy Spirit. Heaven is waiting for "finishers" who will overcome the pressures and temptations of the devil, the world, and their sin nature; all of which are grappling for our attention to distract and entice us to quit.

If this causes you to wonder if you've made the right decision to follow Jesus, you might not be ready to start this race because you haven't counted the cost. When you read the gospel accounts of Jesus' life, he never made it easy for anyone to be his disciple. Sometimes he thinned out the crowd by hitting them with the realities of what it meant to follow him.

He said things like, "No one sets out to build a tower without first estimating the cost. Or no king goes to war against another king unless he sits down and considers whether or not he is able to defeat that king. In the same way, any of you who doesn't give up everything he has cannot be my disciple" (see Luke 14:25-33).

Have you counted the cost? Are you ready to lay down *everything* he'll ask of you to follow him? If, yes, then a wise runner—in a long-distance race—will strip off every article of clothing that might hinder them from running the race well. No long-legged pants, no socks, just feather-weight tops, shorts and shoes to go as fast as they can to finish as strong as they can.

## Honest sinner or deceived pretender?

It's better to be an honest sinner and say, *"I'm not ready for this,"* than to be a deceived church attender who thinks they're saved but were never born again. Just because a person says they've accepted Jesus into their hearts doesn't mean *he's* accepted them.

Sadly, there are many in church who think their prayer of salvation was enough to be saved because someone declared over them, "Praise God! You're saved brother (or sister)! You've asked Jesus into your heart and, therefore, received your salvation. Welcome into the family!"

But *is* that enough?

There are also those in church who think their baptism as an infant, coupled with their parent's faith and prayers, is enough to carry them across the finish line into eternal life. But is that enough?

There are those who believe that regularly attending church is enough to save them as long as they do good deeds. But that's faith in one's works, not faith in the *work* of the cross.

The truth is, none of the above reasons are sufficient for salvation. If the words you prayed were words *without* repentance, words *without* faith or any intention of making a lifelong commitment to Jesus, then they were *only* words—ineffective words that bring no *saving* grace whatsoever.

People who attend church for the cultural, traditional, social or religious aspect of it are playing a dangerous game of deception. They *pretend* they're Christians, *pretend* they love God and might even raise their hands during worship to *pretend* they're honoring him. In truth, they're no different than the gospel accounts of the religious Pharisees whom Jesus said were white-washed graves on the outside, full of dead man's bones on the inside.

The Pharisees and Sadducees were the only people Jesus called hypocrites, *play-actors* who wore masks to depict the character they played in the theatre of religious activities. This is why he said, "Unless your righteousness exceeds the righteousness of the scribes and Pharisees, you'll by no means enter the kingdom of heaven."[15]

Jesus never applied this term to tax collectors or prostitutes who knew they were sinners and made no effort to

---

[15] Matthew 5:20

*pretend* they were righteous before God. They were aware of the condition of their souls more than the Pharisees who condemned them from their platform of piety.

Don't let this be you, praying a prayer of salvation only to save face, or to find a social network for potential clients for your business or to pacify the friend who brought you or to get that friend off your back about going to church.

If this is why you went forward to pray, then you've deceived yourself into thinking your salvation is secured when it is not. It isn't secured because you *acted out* the part of wanting to be saved; God knows your heart and sees the *motives* of your heart.

To be truly saved, your heart must align with the words you confess when you pray a prayer of salvation and ask Jesus to be *Lord* of your life. Otherwise, you're being religious like other hypocrites who are Christians in name only, not reality.

Take a look at the Prayer of Salvation on the last page of this book. If you can pray that prayer with the fullness and sincerity of your heart, understand all that it implies and truly mean it, then you've prayed a prayer of salvation that is genuine.

## Life and Lip

Jesus saves, yes, but he's more than a Savior, he's your Lord. You can't separate the two. You can't have one without the other. If Jesus is not your Lord, he can't be your Savior. Without his lordship over your life, you won't desire to please him and change your ways to align with his. You'll keep your throne and continue to be your own king, your own god. In time, you'll go back to your old ways, erroneously thinking you have an open-ended ticket for eternity's train to the pearly gates—but sadly, you won't.

Jesus must be Lord of your *entire* life. Every part of it—the closets, the hidden drawers—all of it. Otherwise, like the Pharisees in Jesus' time, you'll play the religious game of *pretending* to be a Christian and deceive yourself into believing that you are, when there's nothing about your life to convince others that you really *know* Jesus or that he really knows you. The important question to answer is not, do *you* know Jesus? But does Jesus know *you* (*see* Matthew 7:21-23)?

I've often asked believers this question, "If you were arrested for being a Christian, would there be enough evidence to convict you?" Unbelievers say they don't go to church because of the hypocrites in the church. Though this excuse won't work with God on judgment day, it's true that hypocrites in the church play a significant part in keeping people from God, because of their duplicity. This excuse is given by many for not becoming a Christian and sadly—in many cases—are justified in their perception.

Don't allow your newly professed belief in Jesus to be questioned or seen as hypocritical to those who know you, work around you or live with you. Don't become someone's excuse to reject Jesus and miss their opportunity to receive eternal life. Once you declare you're a Christian to others, they'll watch and wait to see if the two "l's", *life* and *lip,* match up—that is, do you walk the talk?

And though you're just starting to learn how to walk in kingdom life, they'll expect more of you than you will of yourself. It may not seem fair, but the world doesn't play fair.

Our life as a Christian offends and convicts the world of their sins—with or without words. So they look for ways to excuse themselves of sin by accusing the church and Christians of hypocrisy.

## Reading the four gospels

If what I've shared so far hasn't changed your mind and a lifelong devotion to Jesus has been settled in your heart and you intend to finish the race and become a model citizen in Christ's kingdom, then the important thing to do next is to start reading about the life and teachings of Jesus—beginning with the gospel of John in the New Testament.

Each time you read through the stories and narratives, try to visualize its characters and the interaction between Jesus and his targeted audience (religious leaders, sinners, disciples or the sick).

Put yourself back in that time as an observer in the story. Look for nuggets of truth in each teaching of Christ. Ask the Holy Spirit—your internal friend and teacher—to help you grasp the significance of the words you're reading.

I encourage you to live in the gospels for your first months as a Christian, at least until you've read all four of them. After you finish the gospel of John, read Mark, then Matthew and finally, Luke. Take your time to soak in every word Jesus speaks, every deed he performs. Get to know *him*, his heart, his emotions, his integrity, his compassion and his "no-nonsense" approach to completing his mission.

As you read about Jesus, also endeavor to spend systematic, daily reading in the Old Testament book of Proverbs, one chapter at a time.

Proverbs is a gold mine of wisdom for kingdom living today. Get in the habit of underlining, blocking and highlighting any verse that stands out to you and shows you a better way on the theme it addresses.

Also, open the Bible to the middle of its pages where you'll find the book of Psalms. Begin in Psalm One, and read one Psalm a day, blocking and highlighting the "aha" moments that jump out at you. The Psalms are mostly written by King David—a man after God's own heart—and are filled with emotion, passion and reverence for God.

## Not overnight, but a process

Here at the beginning of your heavenly race on earth, you won't be transformed into the image of Christ overnight. By his blood, you'll always stand righteous before God. That work was completed at the cross. His life is already in you by the new birth. But your transformation into Christ likeness is a *process*, a marathon, a lifelong journey.

Oswald Chambers once said, *the **process** is the goal, not the end.*

This process will seem long sometimes because we've accumulated years of wrong thinking, wrong behavior and wrong belief systems. Over time, however, the Holy Spirit will teach us through various ways, including reading the Bible, so as to replace the carnal mind of Adamic thinking with Christ's kingdom thinking.

In the gospels, you'll observe how Jesus spent three-and-a-half years training twelve disciples to change their behavior and worldly views to align with his. That education didn't stop when he died and rose from the dead. He continued the same process in their lives until the day they died or were martyred for their faith and loyal to him.

How rapidly you want to see the Holy Spirit change your thinking to Christ's way of thinking is completely up to you. You'll get what you put into it.

In the case of becoming a *disciple*[16] of the Lord, you'll be transformed as quickly and as much as you give yourself to Bible reading, conversation with God and spending time with him *every* day.

Make time with Jesus a daily priority in your schedule. The more you behold him, the more you will reflect his nature. Don't focus on all you do wrong; focus on what he does right. Then you'll reflect him.

Focusing on *self* and your brokenness will invariably reflect *self*. That's being religious and leads only to a life of perpetual bondage and shame.

Focusing on Jesus, however, and his righteous life, will mirror Christ who lives in you. That's being set free and will lead to a life of peace.

## Your "quiet" place

---

[16] A **disciple** is an unwavering, devoted, "disciplined" learner and follower of the ways, teachings, and life of Christ. They are the most radical among all who call themselves *Christians*, and seek a deeper, intimate relationship with Jesus on a daily basis.

I've always had a *quiet place* where no distraction could occur.

When I first got saved, the best times of the day for concentrated focus on Jesus was early in the *morning* before work, at *noon* during lunch and the last hour of the *night* before bed.

I started my day with Bible reading and prayer, got recharged during lunch and went to sleep at night with God's Word on my mind. That worked well for me and I grew quickly in the Lord.

Find out what works best for you and make such a habit of it you'll feel you've missed a meal—a *spiritual* meal— whenever you skip reading, praying or thinking on the Lord. It's not a sin to miss your quiet time, but it's a good thing to maintain a daily routine as much as possible.

No one can make you do this. It's *you* who decides to make the time and effort. No one can walk your walk with Jesus as diligently as you, except you. And don't rely solely on your brothers or sisters in Christ to help you develop your spiritual disciplines. Approach it as if there were no one else but you, God and the Bible if you want to see significant transformation take place. I made up my mind to do that. Not because I was more spiritual than others, but because I knew it had to begin with my own resolve to give everything I had to Jesus, including my time.

Your *relationship* with God can grow as deep as you want it to. There's no cap, no limit and no end to how close you can get to the Son, how close you can get to the Father and how close you can get to the Holy Spirit—*if* you apply yourself.

The Bible promises that when you draw near to God, he'll draw near to you. It begins every day with you taking that first step. *You* step closer to him, then *he'll* match your steps and move toward you. *Every* time you come to God in prayer, he'll be there because he lives *inside of* you.

Prayer is talking with God like a friend. Include and involve him in everything you do or think about, because he cares about it all and loves being *with* you. Ask him *about* everything *for* everything. And when he responds to your prayers it will most likely be one of three answers: *No, Yes* or *Not Yet*.

## Church attendance—is it enough?

Be careful not to fall into the trap of believing your newfound faith will grow adequately enough by simply attending church. The benefits of growth are certainly there from the inspiring messages and time for *corporate* celebration, prayer and praise to God with his family. It was always the highlight of my week to go to church and be around my brothers and sisters in Christ. I did this Wednesday nights, Sunday mornings and Sunday evenings and loved it! We all wanted the same thing—*more* of Jesus.

But soon I discovered that attending weekly services wasn't the only thing I needed to grow. It was just a small piece of the kingdom life I would come to know.

To think attending church once a week is adequate for spiritual growth is a subtle deception many have come to accept and is dangerous because it lacks accountability and enables indifference- i.e. it justifies people's excuse of being too busy in their schedules to find time for God the rest of the week.

Sunday Christians feel they've done their spiritual duty and paid their respects to God enough to carry them through the week until the next service. In reality, they know nothing more than that, or what it is they're missing out on. We need more.

Look at it from a natural standpoint. You didn't grow up and mature on one cooked meal a week from mom. Ideally, you ate three meals a day. Your spiritual growth requires the same. Feed it *daily*. Feed yourself spiritually like you do now, naturally. You don't want to be a spoon-fed Christian the rest of your life. You want to learn to feed yourself.

As a newborn babe in Christ, you must drink the milk of God's word every day for your growth. Acquaint yourself with the words of Jesus and the

Scriptures because they are written to guide your decisions and approach to life.

The Bible is God's infallible Word, authored by the Holy Spirit, who gave 40 biblical writers the inspired written words of God for us to read. Some writers are mentioned by name, others are anonymous. Some wrote only one book while others like Moses, Solomon, John and Paul wrote more. All the books in the Bible contain the divine, infallible words of God. No other book in the world can lay claim to this.

The Bible is more anointed, more powerful and more inspiring than anything written in history. It is a complete library of God's eternal purposes revealed through ordained letters, chronicles, Psalms, Proverbs and prophecies all pointing to the first and second coming of Jesus Christ, the King of the universe.

## Other steps—Water Baptism and Spirit Baptism

An important step to add to your foundation of salvation is to seek the opportunity to be water baptized into the *name* of the Lord Jesus Christ. Jesus commanded his apostles to do this with every new believer (as is demonstrated in the book of Acts—chapters 2, 8, 10, and 19).

It is in this act that the *name* of your king is branded upon your life as a seal of ownership.

It's like a bride who takes on the name of her bridegroom, legally and ceremonially, on the day of her wedding and makes a public statement to the world that she now belongs to her beloved, and her beloved belongs to her.

It is in the sacramental act[17] of water baptism that invoking the name of the Lord Jesus Christ takes place. It symbolizes the decision to follow him in his *death* (on the cross), his *burial* (in the tomb), and his *resurrection* (from

---

[17] **sacrament**—a religious ceremony or act of the Christian church that is regarded as an outward and visible sign of inward and spiritual divine grace, in particular.

the dead—symbolized by rising up out of the water).

In this act, three things occur. First, we show that we've *died* to our old way of life and nailed it on the cross with Christ. Second, we've *buried* our old, dead man with Christ in the watery grave of baptism and third, we *rise* up out of the water to live a new life in Christ by way of his *resurrected life* in us.

Another important step to add to your foundation is to receive the gift of the Holy Spirit.

When you received the Holy Spirit *within* you, you were born again—i.e. you received the *gift* of salvation. But there's another *gift* of anointing the disciples were to wait for in Jerusalem; a gift that would help them carry out their mission through a demonstration of Christ's kingdom power. This is the same power that Jesus received when the Holy Spirit descended upon him in the form of a dove (see Matthew 3:16; John 1:32-34).

This gift of anointing was imparted to all the new converts in the early church, and he'll give this to you as well. It's in the receiving of this gift that the Holy Spirit comes *upon* you. It is called the *baptism of the Holy Spirit* and was demonstrated in the book of Acts (chapters 2, 8, 10, and 19).

In your **salvation**
—the Holy Spirit comes ***into*** you.

In your **anointing**
—the Holy Spirit comes ***upon*** you.

Seek the help of receiving this gift from someone you know who has it. Perhaps the one who prayed with you might have it or knows someone who does. They'll show you in Scripture what this entails and how it brings more power into your Christian walk.

If you can't find someone to explain either of these two experiences to you, I have books on these two subjects that I highly recommend: *Baptized in Water* and *Baptized with Fire*. They're listed in the back of this book with the website address to purchase them. I encourage you to get them if you'd like to learn how they'll provide you with a greater foundation for your Christian growth in God.

## Saved to be fruit-bearing disciples

It's important to know that Jesus will return someday to examine everything you've done with the gift of salvation you received. You were not only saved *for* a relationship with God and to receive eternal life, you were saved to *become* a fruitful and productive disciple of Jesus Christ.

The Lord wants to make you a world-changer among the broken lives of people who don't know him. You can expect to receive gifts and talents from the Holy Spirit that will assist you in advancing Christ's kingdom on earth through his love, grace and peace demonstrated in your life.

The lost and unbelieving will need to know how to find the same gift of salvation that God gave to you. So you must be equipped to help them.

During your *heavenly race on earth*, it's important to train yourself to answer questions coming from the lost and help them experience what's been revealed to you.

Never forget that you are the *fruit* of someone's prayers, a Christian who befriended you, told you about Jesus, watered the seed of faith that grew inside you and eventually won you to Christ or perhaps someone else reaped the harvest of what another Christian friend or family member had previously sown into you.

You are their *legacy* and can perpetuate it by bearing fruit yourself—just as they had done for the person who assisted them in their spiritual birth. To produce more fruit, a seed must fall into the ground and die until other fruit springs from the ground of that seed.

In time, you'll gradually learn to die to your *self*-life and former way of living. As Christ and his nature increases in you each day, you'll begin to bear more fruit.

When Jesus comes back, he'll look for that fruit as a *return* on his investment. How will he find the investment he left with you when he comes back? Unproductive or multiplied? Will he find you as a *fruitful* Christian or one who buried all he gave? Decide now, because every Christian will give an account someday when Christ returns for what they have done with their Christian walk. Did they finish their race well?

## Not for the faint of heart

As mentioned before, the Christian life you're entering into won't be easy. There'll be days of joy and days of sorrow because we live in a fallen, broken world.

There'll be battles with doubt and a crisis of faith because you have an adversary, the devil, who wants to confuse you and keep you weak in your faith toward God.

There'll be struggles *within*—wrestling with your sin nature—and pressures *without* from those who might hate you, mock you or scoff at you for becoming a wholly, devoted follower of Jesus Christ.

Some might call you a fanatic or an ignorant person who needs "religion" to prop them up because they assume you're too weak to live out your own life.

Others might call you an intolerant bigot or a religious kook—a Jesus freak.

Don't be discouraged by any of this because it comes with the territory of being a Christian, even more so when you grow to the next level of being a *disciple* of Jesus.

When these passive or aggressive actions come against you, count it all joy to suffer as Jesus and the rest of his disciples did in their lives.

Count it all joy because it will only make you stronger in your faith. It will temper you and show you how God will carry you through to the other side of the trial.

Count it all joy because it will teach you things you'd have not learned otherwise.

Count it all joy because every person used mightily by God has gone through fiery trials from their enemies *before* they were ever used in power and strength for God's purposes.

Because people hated, mocked and despised Jesus—some will act the same toward you for believing in him.

They'll accuse you of being *intolerant* of other religions and faiths.

In some countries, they might falsely accuse you of sedition and kill you or imprison you as an enemy of the state if you refuse to renounce Christ as your Lord.

In a free society of the politically correct, they'll accuse you of being an "exclusivist" because the Bible says there is no other *way*, no other *name*, no other *person* who can take you to the Father—other than the *name* and *person* of Jesus Christ (see John 14:6; Acts 4:12).

Always remember when trying times like this occur, *not everyone has faith*. Not everyone will believe in Jesus like you have done.

So be thankful that God has revealed himself to you and opened your eyes to the truth of who he is.

Rejoice also that God imparted *his* faith in you to believe in Jesus, his work on the cross, the cleansing power of his blood and to stand in Christ's righteousness before the Father.

What an amazing thing that you or any of us should be adopted into heaven's family! Legally we have no right to it. Adam and Eve forfeited that right by their disobedience. But God chose to let us be adopted into his family, despite the sins of our *formerly* depraved lives.

He had in place a plan for our redemption through the sacrifice of his Son and the blood that could wash our sins away.

So, if you have authentically and sincerely, from your heart, believed in, confessed with your mouth and received *without* any doubt what Jesus did on the cross for you, then I can confidently say to you, "Welcome to the family!" Your name has been registered into the Lamb's Book of Life in heaven.[18]

**Run well**

Brace yourself now for the greatest adventure of your life. Nothing you've known before will compare to so great a salvation as this.

God the Father loves you. You've entered the unseen realm of an *eternal* life with Christ—a glorious life, a rewarding life. It's the beginning of a great race that will be rewarded when Jesus your Lord and King returns.

Until then, run your race well. There are millions of saints who have gone before you, persevered in their faith, completed their race and are waiting to welcome you home when you cross *your* finish line.

What a glorious day that will be!

---

[18] Revelation 21:27

# ABOUT THE AUTHOR

Jay Zinn became a Christian on January 9, 1972, while serving in the U.S. Air Force in Florida.

During a month-long mission trip to Nicaragua, a calling began to stir in Jay's heart and was later confirmed by a spiritual encounter he had in prayer. Orders then came for a new assignment at an Air Force base in Anchorage, Alaska. This led him into a strong, apostolic church, rich in theology and the gifts of the Spirit.

His calling was confirmed in that church through an elder's prophecy. After three years of equipping and training, the church ordained and sent Jay and his wife, Roseann with a team of five people to plant their first church in Fort Walton Beach, Florida.

After 45 years of pastoring and teaching, Jay has concentrated on his mission to disciple the nations through his Discipleship Group program.

Jay holds a Doctor of Ministry degree and a Ph.D. in Theology from Logos University in Jacksonville, Florida.

He also serves as an apostolic adviser and mentor to pastors and leaders and travels each year, nationally and internationally, to speak at churches and leadership conferences.

On a personal level, regarding Jay's side career, he is a national and international artist in the high-end industry of fine art paintings on canvases of rusted steel.

Jay and his bride, Roseann, reside in Davidson, NC, and have two children and five grandchildren.

# OTHER BOOKS BY JAY ZINN

## *The New Believer's Handbook*
A Guide to Kingdom Culture

## *Baptized with Fire*
A Guide to Understanding
the Baptism of the Holy Spirit

## *Baptized in Water*
A Guide to Understanding
The Importance of Water Baptism

## *The Discipleship Group Series*
A Six-Book Course to Accelerate
Your Spiritual Growth in Christ

---

*You can purchase
these books at:*

**thediscipleshipgroup.com**
*or*
**izeebooks.com**

# A Prayer for Salvation

Lord Jesus, I come before you as a sinner in need of your grace and mercy.

I am depraved and unworthy, lost in my sins which bind my soul and keep me from right standing with the Father.

Only you, Lord, can break these chains of sin by the blood you shed on the cross to redeem my life back to God.

I embrace and believe in the sacrificial work you did for me, knowing that only by your blood—not dead, religious works—can I ever hope to be cleansed and made whole.

I believe that you are God, come in the flesh, who died for me, was buried, and resurrected from the grave after three days and nights.

Forgive me, Lord Jesus, for every sin I've committed in my life against you and others I have wronged. I repent of them and renounce them before you.

Save me, Lord. Deliver me and set me free to serve and worship you forever.

I have counted the cost to follow you and lay my life at your feet, including everything that you and the Bible call sin.

Please be my King, my Lord, and my Master, so that I might be accepted into your heavenly family, as a citizen of your kingdom, a soldier in your army, and be one who will tell the world of your love, your goodness, mercy and grace.

Please save me Lord Jesus. Reign over my life. Holy Spirit come live in my heart to teach me how to love my Lord, and to pursue him with zeal and passion every day of my life, from this day forward.

**~Amen~**